THE PARTING GLASS

The collection of photographs in this book captures the end of an era,
celebrating a way of life that has gone forever in the twilight of the last century;
a toast to the memory of lost Ireland... a parting glass.

" To all friends that e'er I had
they are sorry at my going away,
and of all the sweethearts that e'er I had
they would wish me one more day to stay,
but since it falls unto my lot
that I should rise and you should not,
then fill to me the parting glass...
goodnight and joy be with you all."

(extract from 'The Parting Glass', traditional air)

The Parting Glass

Fragments of our past are scattered all around us along the roads of Ireland. The old folks are gone, along with their hardships, but we can never forget them. We honour them in our memory and think kindly of them, for their gentle ways and soft-spoken voices gave us the gift of the blarney and the ability to charm the world. We inherited their culture, their music, and the sadness of their songs still lives on in our hearts. Now abandoned, decaying homesteads dot the landscape to remind us of they who are gone, and the way we were.

This book manifested itself some thirty years ago, as I drove my old Morris Minor along the west coast of Galway. Unaware of its unfolding creation, I meandered along a country road and came to a halt at an isolated crossroads. The broken rusty signpost pointed one arm towards the Atlantic Ocean, the other towards the ground, as though somehow signifying my destination.

The entrance to a small overgrown boreen beckoned to my right. Mysteriously drawn towards it, I drove down the narrow path past the overhanging briars until I could go no further. What I found there set me on the photographic journey of a lifetime.

The Curse of Emigration

To be born in Ireland is considered a person's first great stroke of luck. If you inherited wealth with it, you hit the jackpot. Realistically, the majority of us lesser mortals were more likely to inherit warts, poverty and a one way ticket for the emigrant ship. Emigration was a part of our culture; from birth it hung over us like a threat. We sang sad songs about the curse of it, how it fell upon unfortunate souls.

We grew up surrounded by heartbreaking tales of our forebears, who were forced to leave with barely enough money for their passage across the perilous oceans. Often we heard of 'American wakes' that celebrated their final farewells before they went off in 'coffin ships' with little hope of ever returning. It was an inherited plague that affected my family for several generations. It was as though you wore a special label, like being earmarked for slaughter.

Yet to a young lad in his teens, bursting with hopes and dreams, emigration promised the only way out. Consequently, many thousands of people were leaving, bound for England, America, Australia, anywhere; there was a great urgency to it all, particularly in the late 1950s, as if the last one to leave might be forced to stay and milk the cows.

Growing up in Ireland I knew that my country had endured many lamentable catastrophes. During my school days I learned of the great famine that starved our forebears. I had read of heroic battles fought and lost. Our teachers coaxed us to memorise ancient events when cruel invaders came pillaging and plundering, but the echo of a more recent war lingered on, touching us in a real sense. It rumbled on like a distant murmur; people still whispered in fear of the English 'Black and Tan' soldiers. As a nation we felt wronged, suffering a legacy of relentless hardships.

By the mid-fifties, the ramifications of what went on before had left the country suffering a kind of drunken aftermath. The countryside bore the scars of continual struggle; poverty showed its ugly face on every roadside. Everything seemed broken and in need of repair, every farm gate held together with bindertwine. The whole country appeared to be bound up, as if our hands were tied behind our backs. The only answer was to leave. Parting from the land of your birth because of poverty required a considerable degree of courage and we respected any adventurous souls who took on this mighty challenge. We honoured anyone who returned triumphantly, especially if they acquired even the modest sprinkling of wealth. We prayed for those who never returned and pitied the unfortunate people who came back penniless; they suffered the shame of failure, for they were now in a worse position than when they first ventured out. For many, that was a failure worse than death; they chose to die begging in some foreign city street, rather than return home to the embarrassment of defeat.

Eight of my uncles had already packed their bags over the years; many were never heard of again. For the remaining family at home this was difficult to comprehend. We struggled to understand how anyone could leave and never bother to write home. We wondered how their lives could have gone so drastically wrong, making them prefer to stay away, keeping quiet. Sometimes we excused them with the notion that they may have been killed fighting in some horrible war. However, there was always the hope that one day they might just come walking down the road or knock on our door unexpectedly. We lived in endless longing, but they never returned.

When someone did return to the parish, there were often moments of glorious excitement as the news spread of the homecoming. I remembered one day someone came running, breathless with astonishment, shouting "Jack Thunder is back!", the name itself made me shudder in anticipation; the magnitude of the news so immense it rebounded in the very air. People abandoned what they were doing, rushing to witness his triumphant return. He was a tall sturdy man, whose reputation as a great character had spanned the intervening years. He came laughing, marching down the road with a huge suitcase balanced on his shoulders. The impact of his momentous homecoming forced grown men to remove their caps, calling out to him as they waved. Some women actually wept with joy. It was a true hero's welcome; you could almost hear the band playing. They were cheering for a man who had played the wild rover for forty years and had returned faithfully home unscathed.

The Leaving

My own departure from Ireland came on a golden late summer evening. The warm sun was tipping over my shoulder as I stepped out courageously to catch the country bus at the crossroads. Carrying a small brown leather suitcase and a winter overcoat, I marched down Blacknock Hill, turning my back on the place that had been my home for the first fifteen years of my life. I was leaving with a mixture of light-headed happiness, deep sadness, and a gripping fear of my unknown future.

There had been no grand farewells, nothing to celebrate; as was customary in our family, it was better to slip away quietly without being noticed. No one actually asked me to leave but circumstances made it partly expected of me. It was understood that one day eventually I would be obliged to sever the umbilical cord with the homeland. It was part of the tradition; most of my schoolfriends expected the same fate.

At home I had said my goodbyes. Aunt Mai and Uncle Tommy walked me to the garden gate without saying much, all the talking had been done, all the decisions had been made. They had kindly reared me in their simple thatched cottage from an early age, after my mother died and my father emigrated. I thought of Mai and Tommy more as parents; they lessened my early misfortunes by helping me to evade life in an orphanage, I would miss them terribly. As we parted I saw the sorrow in their eyes.

I could have stayed, quietly accepting my lot. Ireland had been good to me; my roots were firmly established there. But the possibility of employment in a country place at that time was minimal, it seemed as if you had a choice between joining the priesthood or becoming a farm labourer. Since I was a failed altar boy, my chances of joining the clergy were extremely slim, so enduring the hardships of backbreaking farm-work seemed my only other option. I spent days kneeling in rain-soaked turnip drills wearing wet sacks around my trouser legs, watching the endless stream of waddling cows with bulging udders arrive for milking with monotonous regularity, Enduring it all seemed pointlessly underpaid; consequently neither animal nor land would ever be mine.

Resentment stirred within me as my restlessness increased. I acquired a litany of excuses to justify my departure. The memory of listening to the rats scratching and fighting in the rotting thatch and the fear of them falling on to your bed at night; the chill wind gusting through the keyhole on rainy winter days; staring holy pictures hung on damp distempered walls; creepy candlelit rooms and the lurking presence of our watchful dead ancestors.

I was leaving my hometown, Waterford, affectionately known as 'Lovely Deise', a place of warm hearts famous for making glass, a city of stray dogs, persistent flag sellers and lamenting balladeers; a harbour of bacon factories and aging asylums, importer of jute and cowhide and exporters of sorrowful emigrants.

As I walked towards the station to catch a train bound for the port of Rosslare, the fading evening sky glowed at the edges; soft drizzle began to fall drifting across the city's river. Street lamps shone down with holy lights through yellow clouded cones like frosty morning breath. Misty figures hurried in the dusky light towards the bustling depot. In the distance on the upline tracks, goods trains rattled over well-worn junction points, making way for the expected passenger train.

Entering the station now veiled in rain, I humped my suitcase through the scattered unfortunates waiting to bid their fond farewells. Behind the supporting iron roof columns along the platform, wafts of cigarette smoke rose from unseen individuals; more puffs rising from the centre of small groups standing quietly exchanging little conversation. Older mothers waited with grown-up sons; other women jostled with crying babies, children nervously clutching their mammies' skirts. Some men sat wearily on the edge of bent suitcases, others lay on porters' mail trolleys.

At a momentary glance, my first impression was of a defeated army returning, battle-scarred and beaten, like soldiers struck down in the line of duty sent home to convalesce. But in reality, there were no nurses in white, no crutches, broken limbs or bloodstained bandages; just the wounded expressions of dejected Irishmen leaving their country with saddened eyes.

The train whistled in the distant darkness, signalling its arrival. A bolt of unrest spread among the passengers while porters busied themselves and a red-faced stationmaster appeared, echoing another loud whistle warning everyone to stand well back from the platform edge. Bothered babies sensing the disruption cried even louder, people shifted with unease, pointlessly and uncertainly lifting luggage. Parting lovers clutched each other as if a sentence of death had been passed upon them.

As the train's approach was confirmed by the louder buzzing of the steel tracks, I began to have serious doubts about my decision to leave. Perhaps leaving was not worth all of the pain suffered by my fellow Irishmen down the generations. But the thought of the ridicule I would endure for cowardly changing my mind at the crucial moment forced me onward.

The train finally presented itself, chuffing proudly a few times before freewheeling to its appointed stopping place. It hissed and released steam before lurching uneasily to a halt. A couple of drunks who had over-celebrated their impending adventure swayed and crooned in unison to a laboured rendering of 'The Rose of Mooncoin'. An equally sozzled accordion player accompanied them. The threesome blocked the crowded passageway, totally oblivious to their surroundings. But the rest of the passengers were not so tuneful. Their forlorn expressions reflected my own in the steamy carriage windows. At first glance the packed train looked full of sports supporters on their day out to an All Ireland match at Croke Park, but the carefree laughter was sorely absent. The bulging suitcases piled high in every available space made it abundantly clear this was no Sunday outing. For most of us this was a dark trip into the unknown.

Geographically speaking, if our Emerald Isle was similar to the shape of a bear, as we were taught in school, then I was making my somewhat ungainly exit through Ireland's rear end. Yet I felt united with my fellow passengers, kindred souls with courage and a spark of adventure, plucked from a thousand homes back across the boglands and barren patchwork fields. Young faces from Ireland; from cottages and farms in the hills and valleys; from simple dwellings in narrow boreens; from towns like Dungarvan and Carrick-on-Suir and cities across the whole country. The train carried heavy-hearted individuals, stealing away in the night almost unnoticed, snaking along the winding tracks toward the lonesome ports.

The carriage jolted forward jostling me from my dreaming stance, beginning my journey of a lifetime with a rush of steam. As the train crept away from the dark side of town, I slumped down into my seat. The rain-washed quay swept past in trailing coloured lights, reflecting on the surface of the dripping window pane, and the flickering view slowly faded into a darkness as dense as an ocean of pitch black porter.

My thoughts floated back to my fleeting adolescent years, soaring back in time to some irretrievable moments that were suddenly so precious. Those unforgettable characters that shaped my life, the men I toiled with in the blue-skied cornfields, the women who brought us tea in a bucket to quench our thirst. I would miss the summer flowers of the meadow, the brown-backed field I ploughed listening to the Angelus bell, the girl who saved me a seat in the village hall to watch the magic of film projected on to a crumpled bed-sheet and the taste of my first and only kiss.

Now, as I rushed headlong towards an uncertain future, I forced myself to forget those haunting moments, some of which undoubtedly contributed to my early departure from Ireland. In the years to follow, my mind would recall only the good times, memories which one day would instill the desire to return.

The Return

Fifteen years later I returned with a modest number of achievements. At least I had not fallen by the wayside, begging on some foreign city street. After years of backbreaking work in England, I found myself a softer job, initially as a ship's photographer travelling the world on a luxury liner. Later I was hired to snap the high society faces of the aristocracy. Some of the most beautiful women in Britain and major popstars of the day had posed in front of my lens. I drank afternoon tea with Joan Collins, shared a bag of chips with Rod Stewart and managed to get stuck in a lift with Michael Jackson.

It seemed then that Ireland had little more to offer me, but I duly returned home whenever I could to show my gratitude to my Aunt Mai and Uncle Tommy. During my absence they had lost the old thatched cottage. It became unsafe to live in when the roof threatened to fall. They moved to a new bungalow. Most of the thatched cottages in the parish had collapsed or been abandoned.

On one such summer holiday I drove to the Galway coast, accidentally coming across a narrow lane where I could go no further. What I found there seemed insignificant at first glance; it looked just like any other thatched cottage, similar to many scattered across the landscape. But as I came closer, it looked almost identical to the one I had lived in all those years ago with my aunt and uncle. As I approached the doorway, an old couple suddenly stepped out of it, moving gently and majestically as if stepping out of another age, as though they had been living there since the beginning of time. Their faces were proud and dignified, their clothes looked lovingly homemade. In them I saw truth and a kind-hearted honesty. Old people particularly have attained a greater attachment to the past; they hold the key. They know what went on before, linking us to our ancestors and handing down all that makes us Irish.

The Search

After a warm greeting, they welcomed me into their home. Immediately the overwhelming ambience of the interior, the low thatched ceiling and the smell of smouldering turf gave me a profound sense of loss. Unknowingly this poignant meeting with them instigated a search in me for something. I wasn't yet sure of its meaning. Whenever possible, from that day onwards I began photographing anything remotely connected with the past in Ireland. It might be a broken gate, an old stone wall or an old gramophone. I travelled most of the country, looking, searching.

The sons and daughters of the old couple had emigrated to America; they waited longingly for a homecoming. It reminded me of how little I had seen my own parents. My father did return one hot summer in August in time for the Tramore races. We spoke about his hurling days and he showed me his All Ireland medal. Together we enjoyed a few glorious days on the beach at Bunmahon, then he was gone again.

My mother died of a haemorrhage shortly after the birth of my brother. He too died some weeks later. I was too young to remember much of her, although somewhere in my deepest thoughts I have an image of myself sitting in a carry-chair on the back of a lady's bicycle, the wind blowing a colourful summer skirt which patted my bare knees as we freewheeled downhill in the warm sunshine towards the sparkling sea. I'm not sure of the rider in front of me, but I like to think it was my mother.

I treasure the only photograph I have of her. In it she is standing on a grassy bank holding the handlebars of a sturdy bicycle with her elbows resting on the saddle, and she is smiling. She is captured in a single sepia image in a moment of time, a brief segment of her life caught by a fraction of light that tumbled through a tiny hole in the lens of a box brownie camera. It's all I have of her.

Recently I returned to Annestown beach where some years ago I photographed four heavenly white nuns looking out to sea. I was strangely drawn to the place. I stepped backwards on to a grassy bank overlooking the bay to get a wider angle in my camera view-finder, and there behind me was the very spot where my mother stood all of those years ago. The same rusty gate and the low stone wall were still there, hardly changed in the intervening years. As though I had found a treasure, my fingers touched each familiar stone. My search complete, I stepped on to the same hallowed piece of ground where once long ago my mother stood on a special summer's day and smiled at me in a small box brownie camera.

In the trail of life's journey we are driven by links that unearth our hidden attachments to our past. We occasionally stumble on pivotal moments, that deeply affect the way we are, and the road we must travel.

Richard Fitzgerald 2003

Mother at Annestown beach.

9

Editorial and photograph enquiries: www.richardfitzgerald.com

ISBN 1-901123-43-X

Killarney, Co. Kerry, 1980.

Twilight falls on a land rich in memories and tradition.

Hens, Brownstown, Co. Waterford, 1984.

Peeling paint and decaying walls from a bygone age. The horseshoe on the door is in downward position, a sign of bad luck.

Bunratty, Co. Clare, 1980.

Limewashed cottages were painted in a variety of pastel shades, mainly yellow, pink or light blue.

Hallway at Kitty Power's farm, 1986.

The heroes of the 1916 Easter Uprising are given pride of place in the tranquil hallway.

Shanbally, 1986.

Hens wait expectantly outside the half door.

Co. Mayo, 1970.

Once overworked and often ill-treated, the Irish donkey has become virtually redundant.

Connemara couple, 1970.

The west of Ireland instilled in me a passionate desire to record an age that was fast disappearing.

Achill Island, Co. Mayo, 1980.

The Currach, still used for fishing on the island.

Peatcutters in rainstorm, 1970.   Persistent rain stops work for the day. I met them just after a downpour, returning from the peat bogs.

Achill Island, Co. Mayo, 1985.

The mood of the island is dominated by weather changes.

Derelict cottage, Co. Kerry, 1985.

The beauty of decay shows its striking hues and textures.

Mahon Falls, Co. Waterford, 1993.   The turf-cutting tool is called a 'sleán', the curve on the other end is a cow horn.

Peatcutter's family, Sneem, Co. Kerry, 1971.

Many ancient warriors were bestowed with red hair, a sign of good fortune. This family are waiting with food for their father who is cutting turf nearby, the boy is holding a box of cheese.

Farmhouse, Tramore, Co. Waterford, 1972.

The 'po' or chamberpot, once a
necessity under the bed, is now
used mostly for flower arrangements.

William Quinlan and neighbour Michelle Hewetron, Ross, Co. Waterford, 1986.

The young and the old are natural companions. In Ireland there are no barriers between them. William, who lived alone, had an open house where kindly neighbours kept a watchful eye on his welfare.

Abandoned cart, Co. Galway, 1973.

An aging cart left to decay in a flat-stoned shelter.

Haymakers, Co. Mayo, 1970.

A well-made cock of hay, pleasing to the eye, blends naturally with the landscape.

Co. Kerry, 1970.

Meeting the creamery lorry, numbered milkchurns identify individual farmers.

Peatcutter, Co. Galway, 1971.

We met walking along the road, he spoke mainly in Gaelic.

Kirwan's parlour,
Kilmacthomas, 1990.

A beautiful gramophone from a bygone age, lovely to look at but difficult to carry on a bicycle.

Maggie Kirwan's fireplace, 1992.

A place renowned for its fireside hospitality, it was popular in the old days as a rambling house where everybody was welcomed for a chat.

Billy O'Dwyer, thatcher, Co. Tipperary, 1983.

A reed thatch should last at least ten years.

New thatch, Kilbrien, Co. Waterford, 1991.

A new thatch restores an old cottage to its former glory.

Sullivan's sweetshop, Cahirciveen, Co. Kerry, 1975.

The lady in the window ran this popular corner shop, a favourite stopping off place for children returning home from school.

Backstrand farm, 1993.

The sunshine falls through the trees on a cold Easter Sunday, the cock ran away with the hens.

Weighing scales on a dresser, 1999.

A handy tool to weigh snared rabbits or sweet cans full of blackberries.

36

Butler brothers, Kilclooney, 1992.

Many bachelors in remote areas live on in old farmhouses passed down through several generations. Nicholas and Paddy had a strong bond between them, neither would marry for fear of upsetting the other. I still visit the farm each summer.

Butler's farmhouse, 1991.

Spare bedroom for guests in a fine farmhouse home, unaltered by time.

Butler brothers' bedroom, 1991.   Keeping each other company, the brothers shared the bedroom throughout their lives.

O' Shea's abandoned kitchen, 1986.

A picture of the Pope is left watching over this Catholic dwelling.

Kilclooney parlour, 1980.

The sanctity of the parlour was reserved for special guests only.
In the time of the 'Troubles', secret meetings were held here.

Waterpump, Co. Kilkenny, 1992.

A pump in the yard (and a priest in the family) was a sign of success. Some privately owned wells were dug up to fifty feet deep.

Metalman farmhouse, 1986.

I spent many pleasant evenings with my children around this warm fireside, drinking cocoa and turning the wheel to blow the flames.

Confession at Ballinavouga, Co. Waterford, 1991.

Father Michael Flynn hears the confession of pensioner Jo Walsh,
a comfort to those unable to travel long distances to church.

The Rosary, Co. Waterford, 1991.

Saying the Rosary each evening was commonplace in almost every house in Ireland in the 1950s.

Dancing at the crossroads, 1992.

The Teallach Ceilidh Band provide the music for some lively stepdancing on a Sunday afternoon.

Traditional costume dancers, 1992.

Elaborately costumed young girls keeping up the tradition of Irish dancing.

Doorknocker, Co. Waterford, 1988.

Rust envelopes a once powerful door knocker, an example of Victorian craftsmanship.

Murray's worn piano keys, 1987.

The fingers that spent years tickling these ivory keys may have moved on,
but the mark of the melody remains.

Brothers Michael and Willie O'Brien,
Ballysaggart, Lismore, Co. Waterford, 1991.

The melodion and the fiddle are good companions.

John Cullinan, Dromana,
Cappoquinn, Co. Waterford, 1992.

He was ready in his best suit for
the camera when I arrived while his
extended family watched in the
doorway, waiting with tea and tart.

Comeragh Mountains, Co. Waterford, 1990.

After the wedding, the long road home.

Broken down peat trailer, Co. Galway, 1986.

Someone else's misfortune provided the focal point of this bleak scene, looking along the isolated road
I wondered how long it might take to mend the puncture.

Mackey's farm, 1985.

Layers of paint battle with the rust and the salt sea air.

54

Mackey's farm, 1985.

A strong sturdy bicycle was a godsend in the 1950s.

Travellers' wagons, Bunratty, Co. Clare, 1987.

Elaborately painted wagons that once roamed the roads of Ireland.

Travelling people, Dungarvan, Co. Waterford, 1970.

Part of the Connors family, well known on the roads throughout Munster.

Fidown, Co. Kilkenny, 1987.

On the day that I met these children, their father had gone to visit their mother in hospital.

Travelling children, 1987.

Waiting for their parents to return.

Connor family, Butlerstown, 1970.

The travelling people have not always been treated with respect in Ireland but their love of the wild is admirable. I met this family several times on my travels, they were always kind to me.

Collecting milkchurns, Co. Kerry, 1972.

Numbered milkchurns are collected by the creamery lorry at the crossroads. Before this farmers were obliged to travel long distances, a laborious task that could waste half the day.

Sheepshearer, Mick 'The Tailor', 1995.

A fine looking man from the townland of Cutteen.

Knockenduff, Co. Waterford, 1994

He lived alone with a variety of animals to keep him company.

Mary Keating, 1991.

Religion plays an important part in everyday life.

Louise and kitten, Lyre, 1991.

Growing up in Ireland has its special rewards. In the world of kittens it must be comforting to have a caring friend.

Dunhill Castle, Co. Waterford, 1991.   Well defended by the Powers of Dunhill until 1649, when it was wrecked by the Cromwellian army.

Sneem, Co. Kerry. 1985.

Every goal scorer knows the importance of a well-placed ball.

Co. Clare, 1975.

Sharing the milk by the roadside.

Foxgloves, 1975.

The smell of mown hay in the air, the corncrake echoing in the distance and the memories of long hot summer days.

Blackberry-pickers, 1970.

In the west of Ireland I came upon these blissfully contented children, hurrying home with cups and sweet cans full to the brim. I wonder are they still so happy?

Milking time, 1990.

Cows grazing on the roadside, often referred to as 'the long acre'.

Puck Fair, Co. Kerry, 1970.

Donkeys waiting patiently for a new owner at this popular annual event.

Kerry horse fair, 1970.

Difficult to sell an animal that has been replaced by a tractor.

Sheepshearers, 1995.

On a warm sunny day in June these men from the mountain take a well-earned rest, having just sheared two hundred sheep.

Worn boots, Co. Cork, 1970.

The earthy texture of the old boots on an old wooden table appealed to me.

Currabaha, Co. Waterford, 1999.

Relics from another age.

Keating's farm, Kilrossanty, Co. Waterford, 1990.

Mountain sheep ready for market.

Barndoor keys, 1975.

These once important keys now hang patiently, gathering dust.

Horse drawn mowing machine,
Miss Hanley's farm, Loughdaheen, 1990.

Miss Hanley was a school teacher, cycling fourteen miles
each day to teach in Waterford city.

Doyle's farm, 1986.

This outhouse served many a function, a home for the donkey or young calves.
The hen-laying boxes remain set against the wall.

Mackey's farm washstand, 1983.

Whiter shades of pale, washing facilities await the men from the fields.

Modeligo, Cappoquinn, Co. Waterford, 1989.

Box player Micky Dalton and fiddle player John Foley. I like the blur of the fiddle bow, caught at a speed to complement his fast elbow action. They played until midnight, we drank to each others' health and one for the road

Fiddle, Co. Sligo, 1970.

Hanging fiddle with Stations
of the Cross plaque.

Bodhrán-maker's house, Co. Kerry. 1985.

John B. Keane, the famous Irish writer, directed me to this house.

Kirwan's dog, 1993.

An alert dog is kept busy, this farmhouse has many regular visitors who call for the singing and dancing sessions.

Famine road homestead, 1993.

During the famine, starving people worked for a bowl of soup per day, on a road that went nowhere.

Windowsill, Co. Waterford, 1985.

Discarded relics found in an abandoned home. The newspaper fashion feature is dated 1899.

Tramore, Co. Waterford. 1985.

A bright sunny farm on a Sunday morning in July.

Kitty Power's kitchen, 1985.

The bread was freshly made.
I must have looked at it longingly,
she offered me some with tea.

Doyle's stairs, 1986.

I lived here for the month of August to experience a different lifestyle.

90

Reilly's farmhouse, 1989.

Mai Power fills the teapot during my visit.

Early morning milk, 1990.

As a young boy I took two milk churns to the creamery each day by horse and cart.

Co. Kilkenny, 1995.

A delightful roadside sight, a fine example of a well-cared for cottage.

Potato peeling, Co. Galway, 1970.

The potato will always remind us of the tragic famine. Light for the photograph was provided by opening the front and back doors of the man's cottage. Sadly I've since forgotten this man's name.

Ballinakill, 1990.

The home of John Dunford, still with its original dresser and fine selection of delph plates.

Kilmeaden, Co. Waterford, 1990.

This charming cottage has survived and is now renovated into a two-storey dwelling.

Swiss Cottage, Cahir, Co. Tipperary, 1992.

Built for weekend picnics by the gentry who wanted to emulate those who lived in thatched cottages, a secret tunnel allowed servants to bring food without being seen.

Hens in kitchen, 1992.

Hens take advantage of the open half door.

Maggie Kirwan's dresser, Kilmacthomas, Co. Waterford, 1992.

A popular farm with a history of welcoming strangers.

Farmhouse with Easter Uprising
heroes' picture, 1985.

Yesterday's heroes linger on with pride.

100

Farmhouse kitchen, 1985.

The place was owned by a nice lady, Kitty Power, who made lovely soda bread.

Derelict dresser, 1995.

Abandoned cottage tucked into the mountains where famine struck the hardest.

Abandoned cottage, Dunhill, Co. Waterford, 1980.

A veil of dust shrouds this decaying bedroom.

Holy picture on decaying wall, 1995.

Decaying plaster erodes a religious picture on the wall of an abandoned home.

Ruin, Co. Sligo, 1975.

Scenes of dilapidation marked the end of an era across the whole country.

Abandoned kitchen, 1959.

A recently installed boiler in the kitchen of a fine dwelling house that once had maidservants.

Bathroom, Co. Wexford, 1975.

In its day, this bathroom was probably once state of the art, with a good sized watertank overhead.

Hanging cauldrons. 1989.

A home used by fishermen by the coast near Dungarvan.

Katie O'Brien, Mount Melleray, Co. Waterford, 1991.
She lived without electricity or running water and painted her house black.

Abandoned farm, 1994.

Look at this scene too long and you might fall asleep counting sheep.

Co. Limerick, 1980.

An anxious dog sniffs her
pups, locked inside the shed.

Mackey's farm, 1990.

Reminders of another time with a different lifestyle. The farm is on the south coast overlooking the Atlantic Ocean.

White nuns, Annestown beach,
Co. Waterford, 1975.

It was my mother's favourite beach, where she came to swim. I sat in my car looking out to sea,
suddenly four white nuns appeared looking as though they were about to fly away to heaven.
I quickly took one shot and they were gone.

Storm at Tramore Cove, 1986.

Expecting rough weather, the boats have been removed from the harbour. It was dusk on Christmas Eve, my children were already dreaming of their presents.

Tramore backstrand, 1975.

Having a nun in the family was considered a great honour.

Belfast, 1972.

An angry little boy holds a bottle during troubled times.

Falls Road, Belfast, 1972.

The vehicle was still hot to the touch, the air was heavy with the smell of burning.

Belfast aftermath, 1972.

Birds fly over the smouldering wrecks from the previous night's battles.

Belfast street, 1972

Children at play escape from the horrors of conflict around them.

Refugee camp, Co. Cork, 1971.

A Catholic girl married to a British soldier in Belfast find themselves homeless victims of the conflict.

120

Refugee camp, Co. Cork, 1971.   Hanging blankets provide some privacy between homeless families forced to move out of Belfast.

Inch beach, Co. Kerry, 1970.

The jaunting cart awaits a customer on one of the finest beaches on the west coast.

Holy pictures, 1969.

I married the daughter of a man who was sent to Ireland in the 1930s to sell holy pictures from the family factory in Germany.

Galway coast cottage, 1990.

A ghostly image of the past.

Kilmeaden, Co. Waterford, 1980.

Gathered wildflowers
from the meadow.

125

Banks of the River Suir, Kilkenny, 1980.

The writer of 'The Rose of Mooncoin' melody admired this inspiring view.

Crough, near Mahon Falls, Co. Waterford, 1990.

Bleakness has its own beauty. This is an area famous for its fairy tree, where motor vehicles appear to move mysteriously up the hill without the aid of engine power.

Ring of Kerry landscape, 1980.

The beauty of the landscape in this area is breath-taking.

Ring of Kerry, 1980.

The weather constantly changing with each fast moving cloud, the light reacting like an unfolding movie.

Holy well, Co. Kilkenny, 1992.

A convenient cup, left by a thoughtful person awaits the thirsty traveller.

Comeragh Mountains, 1990.

A spectacular view from the top of Mahon Falls.

Apple market, Waterford City, 1985.

An abundance of fruit at bargain prices before the euro.

Co. Tipperary, 1987.

Watching the world go by, a street scene somewhere in Munster.

Coffinmaker, Ohermong, Cahirciveen, Co. Kerry, 1985.

John T. O'Shea, carpenter, undertaker and jack of all trades, tries a customer for size.
He told me his coffins were the best in the whole country. He tarred the bottoms,
assuring his customers that the deceased would not fall through.

Ballintlea, 1992.

To superstitious people, a black dog on the road could forecast a death in the locality,
in rural communities the loss is known to everyone.

Acknowledgments

I would like to express my sincere thanks to the following
for helping me bring this book together. Firstly, the many
welcoming people I met on my travels in rural Ireland, for
their warmth, kindness and hospitality. Secondly, Richard
Spencer Field for his invaluable help on various trips and
the late night music sessions.

Aislí Madden for design and layout, and all at
John Hinde Ltd. for their appreciation of my work. For her
infinite support and encouragement, I owe special
gratitude to my wife Louise who contributed in numerous
ways and to my children Giles, Anna, Maria, and Michael,
for sharing some of the experiences and adventures
down many long boreens.

Published 2003 by John Hinde Ltd. 71-73 Heather Road, Dublin 18, Ireland. Printed in China. www.johnhinde.com